Leet's Christmas

Leet's Christmas

Elithe Hamilton Kirkland

Illustrated by Toni Thomas

University of North Texas Press
Denton, Texas

Requests for permission to reproduce material from this work
should be sent to:
Permissions
University of North Texas Press
P.O. Box 13856
Denton, TX 76203

The paper in this book meets the minimum requirements of the
American National Standard for Permanence of paper for
Printed Library Materials, Z39.48.1984.

Library of Congress Cataloging-in-Publication Data

Kirkland, Elithe Hamilton.
    Leet's Christmas / Elithe Hamilton Kirkland.
        p.   cm.
    ISBN 1-57441-014-8 (cloth : alk. paper)
    1. Kirkland, Elithe Hamilton—Childhood and youth.
2. Women authors, American—20th century—Biography.
3. Texas—Social life and customs. 4. Christmas—Texas.
5. Family—Texas. I. Title.

PS3561.I6896Z469   1996
813'.54—dc20
[B]   96-16221
                                                         CIP

To Elihu,

my grandfather

$\mathcal{G}$randfather Daniel Elihu

Purcell would not be caught dead in a

Santa Claus suit! He was too carefully self-

chiseled into what he was ever to accept

any kind of masquerade.

He was the acknowledged seat of power

to his grandchildren at Christmas time as

at all other times; but his personality took

on an added dimension at this special sea-

son which enhanced their excitement. He

was for sure the Grand Arbiter with that

wondrous Force called Santa Claus.

Daniel Elihu was straight-shouldered, handsomely mustached, with the firm tread of authority in his step—more the type to serve on the Federal Grand Jury in the faraway capital city of Austin—which he did.

The ancestral Purcell blood had flowed Texas-strong through his veins since the days of the Republic, and his corpuscles were a mix of Fayette County history,

Burnet County cedar, and Coleman County daring, for he had brought his family of wife and grown children to this pioneer arena in 1900 to settle on a rich section of farm and grazing land.

Leet (circa five years) was a favorite grandchild, and the Christmas season her favorite time to visit her grandparents through the awesome period of preparation for the family reunion on into the climax of Christmas Day.

To appreciate Leet's status in her world (circa 1912), you must know that she had never been to school, was spellbound when she was told fairy stories or folk tales, and adored Daisy her china-headed doll. Daisy, like Leet, was an only child, her all-porcelain head animated with black hair, very blue eyes, and delicate oriental features, attached to a shapely body (well, shapely enough for those times) of cloth stuffed with straw. Leet's home was a three-room

white frame house; her "castle" was the big two storied, doublechimneyed white and green Purcell ranch house.

The rural setting in which she thrived was backdrop for heady adventures where her horse came to her call, her dog performed tricks according to her instructions, and the kittens and baby chicks were more fun than crackerjacks. There were high points when Grandmother Purcell, full-skirted and spirited as the mare she rode,

would mount to her side-saddle and lift
her eager grandchild up behind her to cling
to her waist while she galloped away to
visit with a neighbor; or, in a milder dis-
play of energy, would invite Leet to go with
her to the milking pen—which meant being
allowed to perch on the green board fence
until Grandmother brought her a large
enamel mug filled to overflowing with
frothy milk from the brown Swiss cow.
They would both laugh at the foam left all

over her face, for the mug was face-size.

You would also have to realize that Leet was an avid watcher of the traditional mixing of the golden eggnog in the big crystal bowl, the ritual and recipe having advanced somehow to the land of limited-living-waters from the fertile deep South.

This was not an age of freewheeling grandchildren who take over the command post at Christmas wherever they may be. Grandfather Purcell saw to it that his

sprouting descendents were suitably
trained not to disturb the farm animals, not
to climb the big straw stack (a tempting
mountain of beckoning)—for this would
break the crust and spoil the fodder, not to
stray into lots and pens until old enough to
help with the chores. Grandmother kept
little girl hands out of mischief with sifting
flour, stirring batter, grinding coffee, bringing in wood for the cookstove. Yet there
was always time for games and tumbling
on the Bermuda grass lawn.

24

Childhood expectations at Christmas
included once-a-year fruit and nut treats.
Those not native grown had to be freighted
in to the county seat by wagon or the new
extension of the Santa Fe Railway; apples,
oranges, bananas, walnuts, Brazil nuts,
even coconuts were a part of the Santa
bounty. Grandfather would install a whole
stalk of bananas on a wire in the cellar—the
fragrance mixed with that of brandied
peaches was of such unique pleasure to

Leet that she would slip into the cellar
unwatched and take deep breaths until she
was dizzy—but pluck a banana? Never!
Only Grandfather and Grandmother did
that.

As for toys, the stockings would likely
hold a packet of little firecrackers, one or
two marvelous starry sparklers, perhaps a
top or a ball; sometimes something grand
like a red wagon or a new doll would grace
the hearth. Leet was hoping Santa would

bring a doll buggy or bed for Daisy and just maybe a set of painted playhouse tin dishes.

Grandfather provided all the goodies, but it was up to his children and in-laws to furnish the toys. The Purcell grandchildren had discovered to their joy that, in one respect, grandfather stepped entirely out of character in preparations for Christmas morning.

Leet was determined to take early

28

advantage of this departure. It was still three very long days until the morning of mornings.

She found her grandfather, looking serious and contemplative, seated in his rocking chair before the living room fireplace. To Leet this place was like a breathing center in her castle. It was the fireplace designated for Santa's delivery route. On the mantle, the Seth Thomas clock was a never sleeping presence of ticking and

striking, and the framework for a firebox of native rock was made of heavy lumber painted a rich creamy brown. The hearth was an artistic spread of flagstones.

Leet rushed out to the carriage house toolbox, made a quick choice and hurried back to confront the "Arbiter" with a heavy hammer and a very long nail. (To deface a painted surface on the Purcell premises was a violation ranked along with sassing an elder. But in celebrating the Birth of the

Savior, even Daniel Elihu Purcell must make concessions.)

"A little early, aren't you, Leet?"

She didn't reply, but she noted that his mustache twitched in a barely suppressed smile.

She ventured a beseeching smile in response.

"Well, now . . ." he accepted the hammer and nail. The time he took to look them over worried Leet. He inquired, "Have you decided where you want to hang it?"

She went to the brown panel and mea-
sured from the stocking she was carrying.
The surface was pocked with nail holes
painted over from the year before.

She put her finger on the spot where she
wanted the nail to go.

"Goodness me, girl, you're fudging on
Santa Claus. That's not your stocking,
that's your Mama's. Do you think that's
fair to Santa Claus? He might even fill it up
with surprises for your mama."

Leet blushed and hung her head.

"Oh well. I think most likely he'll understand. And besides, we'd want him to have plenty of room and not get things mixed up on the hearth."

He got up to set the nail with a firm whack or two, then handed the hammer back to Leet.

She held it awkwardly. The nail was not as far in as it should be.

"You can finish driving it in. Have at it."

She grasped the heavy pounder with both hands and swung out bravely . . . Hit! . . . Miss!! . . .The nail hadn't budged. So! Hit! Miss!! Hit! Miss!! Miss!!

"Take it easy, girl. Get a firm grip and hit with all your might."

She raised the hammer above her head and struck with all the force her five-year-old muscles could muster. Bam!!! Her blow caused Seth Thomas to tremble . . . and left a forever full print of the hammer face in the woodwork!

She turned to her grandfather in consternation, panting and red-faced.

He threw back his head in a big guffaw!

Grandfather was certainly different at Christmas time!

The next day Grandfather was up early and hitching the matched team to the shiny black surrey for a trip to the county seat. He would spend most of the day in town selecting the perishable supplies for stockings and Christmas dinner. Leet watched

every step of the process, yearning for the time when she would be big enough to help with all the mysteries of bright brass buckles and fresh dressed black leather.

She stayed at the hitching post until he came out dressed in his three-piece suit with his gold watch pocketed, the beautiful gold chain spread across his chest. After he took the loop from the hitching post, her big moment of the day was upon her. It hadn't happened last Christmas, but some-

thing in the air between her and Grandfather made her feel it would happen now.
And it did. He asked her to hold the horses
while he took his place on the front seat.
Once there, he took out his watch, a golden
globe gleaming in the morning sun, and
studied it gravely to check the time of
departure. She caught her breath in delight.
He signaled her to step back. A wave and a
smile of shared confidence and he was off
at a fast clip. She kept waving until he was

out of sight. The whole was a little secret drama in which each knew that the other was playing to a devoted audience of one.

Her experience in the afternoon was at the other end of that sensitive emotional arc structured into early childhood when eagerness can catapult into disaster. It happened with Uncle Austin, the handsome young bachelor of the family, who teased and laughed a lot. To Leet he was the living prince of fairy tales.

He had taken a trip to town also, leaving before dawn—there were ten miles to be covered and a young man had different kinds of business to see to than the head of a household. When he arrived home, he stopped the buggy at the back door and Leet raced out to open the yard gate, for he would be bringing in packages. And so he was—in one hand a loaded basket and in the other the bottle of Four Roses that was as much a part of the traditional Christmas

eggnog as eggs and whipped cream. He laughed and held out the unpackaged bottle to show Leet. The Four Red Roses shining forth in their gold and green embellishment were gorgeous to behold! She laughed too, and held out her hands for the privilege of carrying it in to Grandmother.

How could it possibly have come to pass that her small hands had not tightened enough around the slick bottle? It

slipped from her grasp and hit the flagstones with a shattering of glass and a great
spatter of spirits in every direction. She
was stricken with the horror of it. She
glanced up at Uncle Austin's face in time to
receive the shock of his dismay, which he
quickly converted to a smile of forgiveness.

In later years she could evoke no recall
on any further details of the disaster. Was
the amnesia immediate and permanent?
Was there any other consternation in the

household? Who cleaned up the mess? Was there another bottle of Four Roses for the eggnog? Was Uncle Austin's dismay so deeply etched into her consciousness because he had an extra bottle saved for himself that now must be placed on the altar of tradition? She knows only that even if she should make it in this life far beyond the year 2000, she would continue to clutch with a vice-like grip any bottle of Four Roses that might come into her hands as

the old family eggnog recipe continued to
make its rounds on Christmas Day.

Leet's Christmas angel must have been
abroad at the time, for by Christmas morning no conscious scars shadowed the thrills
of discovery. There were no toy dishes, no
buggy or bed for Daisy, but something
more wonderful had happened. There sat
Daisy under the bulging Christmas stocking. She no longer wore her baby clothes,
but was resplendent in red flannel coat and

woolly cap, red stockings and black laced boots. A blue velvet dress peeped out from under her coat and the box beside her looked like a doll's trunk in its white paint and brass trimmings.

Leet raised the lid and it was filled from top to bottom with a whole wardrobe for Daisy, all as perfectly patterned and stitched as her own clothes. She had two minds working at once. Santa Claus was certainly full of surprises! How did he

arrange with Mama and Dad to make all
this for Daisy? Perhaps the fairy folk
helped out.

So later the eggnog was served from the
big crystal bowl as usual, and a few hours
after that the Christmas feast was spread.
The turkey replaced the eggnog at center
position on the dining table. Around it
were such attributes as an enormous spiral
of whipped potatoes with butter melting
into rivulets along the creases as it waited

for the cornbread dressing and giblet gravy; a deep platter of crusted cabbage (boiled in chunks and while still solid covered with thick sweet cream and placed in the oven); thick flaky biscuits heaped high on an oversize plate and set close beside a block of yellow butter fresh from the mould that made a floral imprint on top; gleaming jellies, large spiced peach pickles, small brandied peaches from the native tree at the back door, canned with the thick

skin left on (sneak a whole one into your mouth to separate from the seed, close your eyes in reverence for the flavor!). And desserts? Jeff Davis chess pie, chocolate meringue pie, pumpkin pie, spice cake, pound cake, layered cakes—chocolate and fresh coconut—or dark fruitcakes with whipped cream.

The elders sat at the dining table, their topics of conversation ranging from positions, politics and religion to the vagaries

of weather, horse racing, hunting dogs, wolf chases, sheep losses, pasture conditions and cattle rustling. As they ate and talked, they sipped hot coffee (brewed in a big pot from beans fresh roasted and ground). Some cooled it in the saucer. Daniel Elihu Purcell had a mustache cup. The children ate at the long table in the kitchen, giggling and teasing, their mothers periodically refilling their plates and correcting their manners.

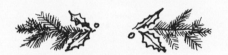

$\mathscr{B}$y evening of the day
after Christmas, families had departed, all
things seemed stilled, and Leet was the
only child around. She retreated to one of
her favorite nooks in the winter sun, next
to the south chimney in the corner made
with the house. On a pad of dry Bermuda
she settled with Daisy in her arms. Her
timing was intentional. Soon from Grandfather's very private room, just over her
head on the second floor, came the sounds

she was expecting. He was sounding his
do-re-mes, tuning up for a practice session
with his Sacred Harp song book. He had
showed it to her one time, explaining how
the shape of each note on the page repre-
sented a tone which he called do-re-me-fa-
so-la-ti-do. . . . She waited. Soon he would
sing a song. The big yellow striped barn cat
Samson lay down beside her and began a
loud ribby purring.

"Shh . . . !" she said to him. "Listen,
Grandfather is about to sing."

60

On Jordan's stormy banks I stand
And cast a wish-ful eye (wishful eye)
To Canaan's fair and hap-py land,
Where my pos-ses-sions lie

CHORUS:
Oh, who will come and go with me?
I am bound for the promised land;
(promised land)
Oh, who will come and go with me?
I am bound for the promised land,
(promised land).

And Leet slipped into a state of bliss

only a child could attain.

BRIGHT PROSPECT.

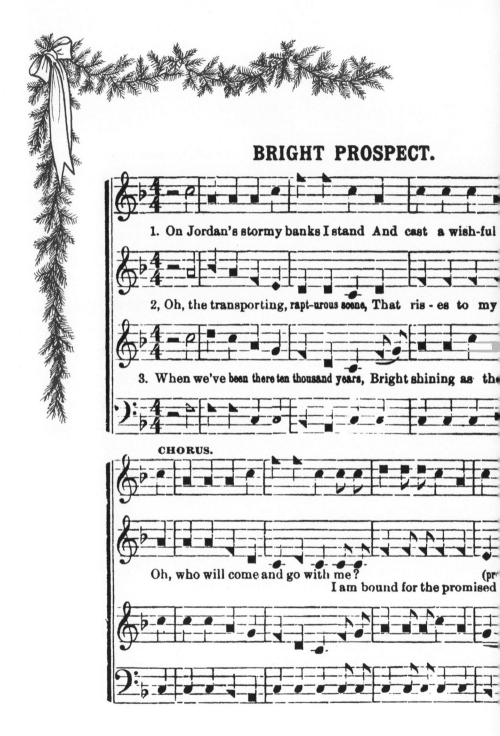

1. On Jordan's stormy banks I stand And cast a wish-ful

2, Oh, the transporting, rapt-urous scene, That ris - es to my

3. When we've been there ten thousand years, Bright shining as the

CHORUS.

Oh, who will come and go with me?   (pr

I am bound for the promised

"Bright Prospect," *The Sacred Harp*, W. M. Cooper & Co., Dothan, Ala. 1909.

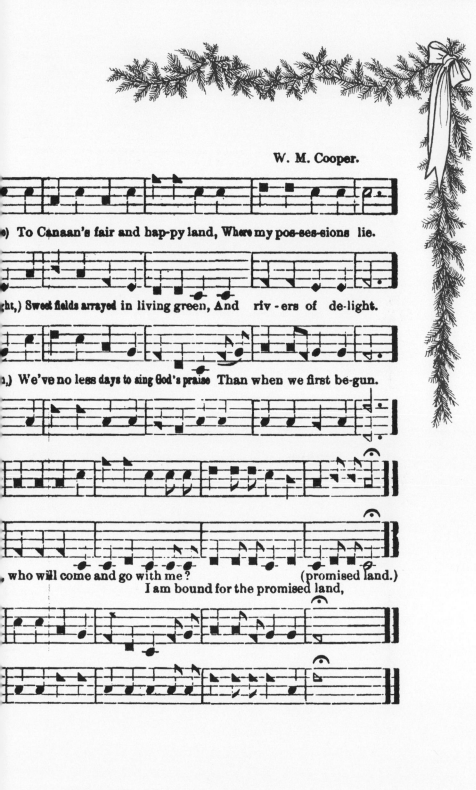

W. M. Cooper.

) To Canaan's fair and hap-py land, Where my pos-ses-sions lie.

ght,) Sweet fields arrayed in living green, And riv-ers of de-light.

,) We've no less days to sing God's praise Than when we first be-gun.

, who will come and go with me? (promised land.)

I am bound for the promised land,